ALL AROUND THE WORLD
CZECH REPUBLIC

by Kristine Spanier, MLIS

Ideas for Parents and Teachers

Pogo Books let children practice reading informational text while introducing them to nonfiction features such as headings, labels, sidebars, maps, and diagrams, as well as a table of contents, glossary, and index.

Carefully leveled text with a strong photo match offers early fluent readers the support they need to succeed.

Before Reading
- "Walk" through the book and point out the various nonfiction features. Ask the student what purpose each feature serves.
- Look at the glossary together. Read and discuss the words.

Read the Book
- Have the child read the book independently.
- Invite him or her to list questions that arise from reading.

After Reading
- Discuss the child's questions. Talk about how he or she might find answers to those questions.
- Prompt the child to think more. Ask: The Czech Republic is landlocked. Can you name any other landlocked countries?

Pogo Books are published by Jump!
5357 Penn Avenue South
Minneapolis, MN 55419
www.jumplibrary.com

Copyright © 2023 Jump!
International copyright reserved in all countries. No part of this book may be reproduced in any form without written permission from the publisher.

Library of Congress Cataloging-in-Publication Data

Names: Spanier, Kristine, author.
Title: Czech Republic / by Kristine Spanier, MLIS.
Description: Minneapolis, MN: Jump!, Inc., [2023]
Series: All around the world | Includes index.
Audience: Ages 7-10
Identifiers: LCCN 2022023226 (print)
LCCN 2022023227 (ebook)
ISBN 9798885241946 (hardcover)
ISBN 9798885241953 (paperback)
ISBN 9798885241960 (ebook)
Subjects: LCSH: Czech Republic—Juvenile literature.
Classification: LCC DB2011 .S63 2022 (print)
LCC DB2011 (ebook)
DDC 943.71—dc23/eng/20220519
LC record available at https://lccn.loc.gov/2022023226
LC ebook record available at https://lccn.loc.gov/2022023227

Editor: Jenna Gleisner
Designer: Molly Ballanger

Photo Credits: Noppasin Wongchum/Shutterstock, cover; CTK/Alamy, 1, 20-21; Pixfiction/Shutterstock, 3; Kletr/Shutterstock, 4; Vaclav Sonnek/Dreamstime, 5; Patryk Kosmider/Shutterstock, 6-7; givaga/Shutterstock, 8-9; WildlifeWorld/Shutterstock, 10-11tl; Martin Prochazkacz/Shutterstock, 10-11tr; Vladimir Muller/Shutterstock, 10-11bl; Philip Bird/SuperStock, 10-11br; Peteri/Shutterstock, 12; Herrndorff image/Shutterstock, 13; V_E/Shutterstock, 14-15; CentralITAlliance/iStock, 16-17; Andrey Starostin/Shutterstock, 18 (schnitzel); Moving Moment/Shutterstock, 18 (goulash); Jan_Mach/Shutterstock, 18 (žemlovka); Cum Okolo/Alamy, 19; Eva Rozkosova/Shutterstock, 23.

Printed in the United States of America at Corporate Graphics in North Mankato, Minnesota.

TABLE OF CONTENTS

CHAPTER 1
Landlocked 4

CHAPTER 2
Daily Life 12

CHAPTER 3
Art, Food, and Festivals 18

QUICK FACTS & TOOLS
At a Glance 22
Glossary 23
Index 24
To Learn More 24

CHAPTER 1
LANDLOCKED

Welcome to the Czech Republic! Would you like to explore a castle? King Charles IV lived in Karlštejn Castle more than 650 years ago.

Karlštejn Castle

The Czech Republic is in Central Europe. It is **landlocked**. Germany and Poland are north. The Oder River connects to the Baltic Sea. Austria and Slovakia are south.

Oder River

The Giant Mountains form part of the border with Poland. Mount Sněžka is here. It is the country's highest point. It rises 5,256 feet (1,602 meters).

> **DID YOU KNOW?**
>
> Czechoslovakia was once a country. In 1993, it split into two countries. They are the Czech Republic and Slovakia. The Czech Republic is also known as Czechia.

Prague is the largest city. It sits on both sides of the Vltava River. From 1402 to 1841, there was only one bridge that crossed the river. It was Charles Bridge. Now, there are 17 bridges!

Charles Bridge

Vltava River

TAKE A LOOK!

Prague is in Bohemia. This is one of the Czech Republic's three **regions**. It is the largest. Moravia and Silesia are the other two. Take a look!

Little owls live in the country's grasslands. They grow just eight inches (20 centimeters) tall. Wild boars live in the Šumava Mountains. Lynx roam the forests. Mink find homes near the rivers.

CHAPTER 1

CHAPTER 2
DAILY LIFE

The mild **climate** in the south is good for growing **crops**. Farmers grow wheat, barley, oats, and potatoes. They raise **livestock** like cattle, sheep, and pigs.

wheat field

There are many ways to earn money in the Czech Republic. Some people build vehicles.

CHAPTER 2 | 13

Prague is the **capital**. It is where the government meets. A prime minister and a president lead the country.

The president can choose to live in the Prague Castle. It is a **complex** of buildings. Built more than 1,000 years ago, it is the largest **ancient** castle in the world!

WHAT DO YOU THINK?

The Czech Republic joined the **North Atlantic Treaty Organization (NATO)** in 1999. It joined the **European Union (EU)** in 2004. Both groups protect countries' freedom. Do you think these groups are important? Why or why not?

Children here start school by age six. They attend until they turn 16. Many go on to secondary school. These schools prepare students for college or jobs.

CHAPTER 3
ART, FOOD, AND FESTIVALS

Lunch is the biggest meal of the day. Schnitzel is breaded pork. Goulash is pork stew. Would you like something sweet? Žemlovka is bread pudding. It is made with sweet milk and fruit.

schnitzel

goulash

žemlovka

Have you seen **glassblowing**? Artists have been making glass objects in Bohemia for more than 1,000 years.

glass

CHAPTER 3

Many festivals take place in spring. The Ride of the Kings is one. People dress in **traditional** clothing and ride horses. They eat special foods. They play traditional music.

There is much to see in the Czech Republic! Would you like to visit?

WHAT DO YOU THINK?

One boy is chosen for the Ride of the Kings. He gets to act as king. Others ride their horses with him. Would you like to be chosen as king? Why or why not?

QUICK FACTS & TOOLS

AT A GLANCE

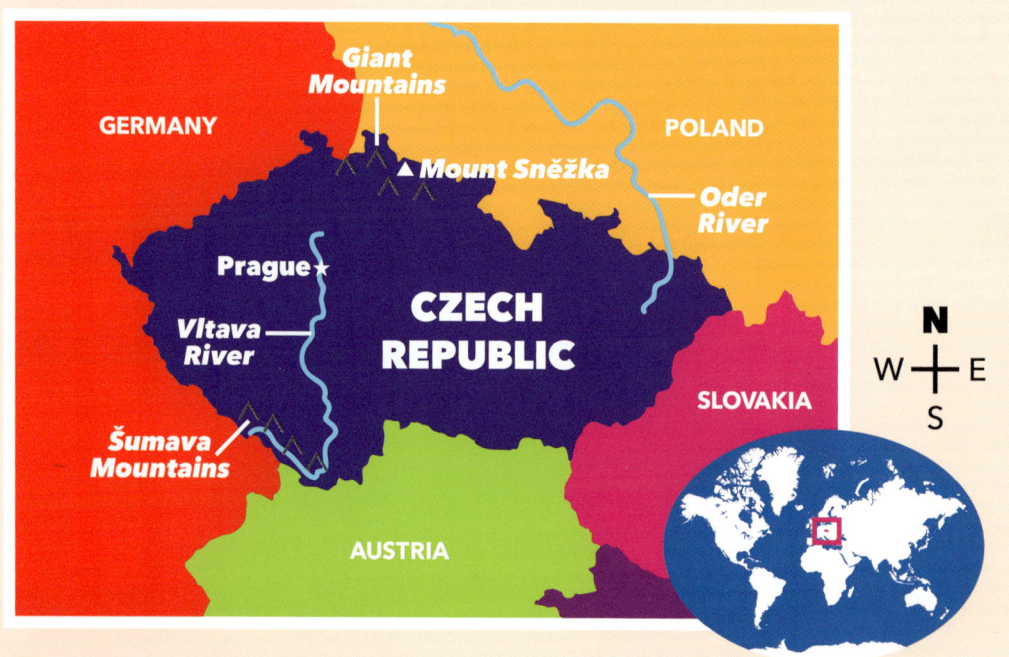

CZECH REPUBLIC

Location: Central Europe

Size: 30,451 square miles (78,867 square kilometers)

Population: 10,705,384 (2022 estimate)

Capital: Prague

Type of Government: parliamentary republic

Languages: Czech (official), Slovak

Exports: cars and vehicle parts, computers, broadcasting equipment

Currency: Czech koruna

GLOSSARY

ancient: Belonging to a period long ago.

capital: A city where government leaders meet.

climate: The weather typical of a certain place over a long period of time.

complex: A group of buildings that are near each other and are used for similar purposes.

crops: Plants grown for food.

European Union (EU): A group of European countries that have joined together to encourage economic and political cooperation.

glassblowing: The art of shaping melted glass by blowing air into it through a tube.

landlocked: Not having any borders that touch the sea.

livestock: Animals that are kept or raised on a farm or ranch.

North Atlantic Treaty Organization (NATO): An organization of countries that have agreed to give each other military help. This group includes the United States, Canada, and some countries in Europe.

regions: General areas or specific districts or territories.

traditional: Having to do with the customs, beliefs, or activities that are handed down from one generation to the next.

Czech Republic's currency

INDEX

animals 11
Baltic Sea 5
Central Europe 5
Charles Bridge 8
climate 12
crops 12
Czechoslovakia 6
European Union 15
food 18, 21
Giant Mountains 6
glassblowing 19
government 15
Karlštejn Castle 4
landlocked 5
livestock 12
Mount Sněžka 6
North Atlantic Treaty Organization 15
Oder River 5
Prague 8, 9, 15
Prague Castle 15
regions 9, 19
Ride of the Kings 21
school 16
Šumava Mountains 11
vehicles 13
Vltava River 8

TO LEARN MORE

Finding more information is as easy as 1, 2, 3.

❶ Go to www.factsurfer.com
❷ Enter "CzechRepublic" into the search box.
❸ Choose your book to see a list of websites.